Aberdeenshire Library and Information Service
www.aberdeenshire.gov.uk/libraries
Renewals Hotline 01224 661511

HARRISON, Paul

Big cats

UP CLOSE

Big Cats

PAUL HARRISON

W
FRANKLIN WATTS
LONDON·SYDNEY

Published in 2009 by Franklin Watts

Copyright © 2009 Arcturus Publishing Limited

Franklin Watts
338 Euston Road
London NW1 3BH

Franklin Watts Australia
Level 17/207 Kent Street
Sydney, NSW 2000

Author: Paul Harrison
Editor: Fiona Tulloch
Designers: Trevor Cook, Sally Henry

Picture credits: Ardea London Ltd: 4, 5, 8, 10 top and bottom, 11 bottom, 13 lower top; Bruce Coleman: 16 top, 18 and 19 bottom and back cover; Macduff Everton/Corbis: 17 bottom; Nature Picture Library: title page, 6, 7 top, 19 top left, 20 top and bottom; NHPA: 2, 5 bottom right, 10 middle, 12 bottom, 14 bottom, 16 bottom; Oxford Scientific (OSF)/Photolibrary.com: 5 top, 9 top, 13 bottom right and bottom, 15, 18 top, 21 top; Science Photo Library: front cover and 21; The Bridgeman Art Library: 19 top right.

A CIP catalogue record for this book is available from the British Library

Dewey number: 599.75

ISBN: 978-0-7496-9213-1
SL000951EN

Printed in China

Franklin Watts is a division of Hachette Children's Books, an Hachette UK Company
www.hachette.co.uk

Contents

What Is a Big Cat?

Today there are over 30 *species* of cat. The group known as big cats is made up of tigers, lions, leopards, jaguars, cheetahs and cougars.

Big cats are found in the wild on the continents of North and South America, Africa and Asia.

WHAT BIG TEETH YOU HAVE

The many species of *sabre*-toothed cat lived mainly in North and South America. Their big pointy teeth could grow to more than 30 centimetres long. They hung out of the mouth when it was closed. These cats died out around 10 thousand years ago.

SAME DIFFERENCE

Cats of all sizes have acute senses of smell and sight, and they all like to keep clean. They're all *carnivores*, too – and the bigger the cat, the more it eats.

UNDER THREAT

Many species of big cat are threatened with *extinction* by hunters, as well as the loss of their *habitat*.

WHAT'S BEING DONE?

One way to help is to show people how important big cats are to the local economy. A dead cat can bring big money for *poachers*, but a live cat can bring in much more money from rich tourists.

Tigers

The tiger is the biggest of all the big cats, and the Siberian tiger is the biggest of all. It can grow up to 4 metres long.

Tigers are found in India, Siberia, and South-East Asia.

GOOD MOTHER

Tigers are solitary creatures except when a mother tiger is raising her young. The cubs stay with their mothers for around 2 years until they leave to find their own territories. During those early years, the mother will teach her cubs how to survive. They learn to stalk and hunt *prey* – if they don't eat, they won't survive.

MAN HUNTER

No-one lives in the Sunderban region of Bengal, in India, but people go there to hunt. Tigers kill people there every year. Knowing that tigers like to sneak up on their prey, the locals wear masks on the back of their heads. A tiger creeping up from behind will think it has been spotted.

A DIFFERENT STRIPE

No two tigers have the same pattern. Every one is different, like our fingerprints!

FANCY A DIP?

Like pet cats, some big cats hate the water. Not the tiger though. It likes nothing better than a relaxing swim in a cool river or pond.

Lions

The lion is often called the king of the beasts. In their own territories, they're certainly kings of all they survey.

SOCIABLE CATS

Lions are social animals, which is unusual in the cat world. They are the only cats to live in family groups, which are called prides.

VANISHING SPOTS

Strangely, lion cubs are born with spots. As the cubs get older, the spots disappear.

Lions are now only found in certain parts of Africa and India.

TEAM WORK

Lions are not the fastest of the big cats. Their prey, such as gazelles and zebras, can be very quick indeed. Lions hunt as a team. Generally, it's the lionesses that do all the hunting. When it comes to eating it's the males who eat first -- not very fair!

SLIM PICKINGS

It's a tough life for cubs. They are always last to feed after a kill. Some cubs can starve to death if there's not enough meat to go round.

HOME GUARD

While the females do most of the hunting, the largest males take care of defending the pride against intruders.

MANE ATTRACTION

Male lions are the only members of the cat family to have a mane. Many scientists believe it's for making the lion look good. The darker the lion's mane, the more attractive the male is to females.

Leopards

T he leopard can live in all sorts of *environments* and hunts many types of animal, from lizards to baby giraffes.

Leopards are found in Africa, India, Siberia, China and Indonesia.

TREES

Leopards are great climbers and spend a lot of time up trees either sleeping or hunting. Trees are a great place for leopards to hide their food. After making a kill, leopards carry the bodies into trees for safe-keeping.

HEAVY MEAL

It takes great strength for the leopard to lift the kill into the safety of a tree. It can weigh up to three times the cat's own body weight!

DIFFERENT VARIETIES

There are more than 20 species of leopard, and they come in all sorts of shapes and sizes. The clouded leopard of the Indonesian islands and the snow leopard of Siberia are different enough from normal leopards to be classed as two species.

DISAPPEARING TRICK

A leopard's odd patterning of rings and spots, called rosettes, is excellent for helping it hide in trees or long grass.

FOLLOW ME

To help their cubs find them in spite of the *camouflage*, leopards have bright white spots behind their ears.

BLACK PANTHER

Some leopards are born almost completely black in colour and are known as panthers. More panthers are born in areas with thick jungles.

BLACK AND BLACKER

Look closely at the coat of a panther, and you'll see the faint spots and rings of the leopard.

Jaguars

Jaguars are found in South and Central America, also in south-western parts of North America.

The greatest South American *predator* is the jaguar. Like the leopard, the jaguar is a stealthy night hunter, using its excellent night-vision to track prey.

HEADACHE

Unlike most big cats, which bite the neck of their prey, the jaguar kills by using its powerful jaws and sharp teeth to bite the head.

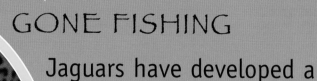

GONE FISHING

Jaguars have developed a great method of catching fish! The cat waits by the water and splashes the surface with its tail. For some reason, this attracts fish which are scooped out of the water with the jaguar's paws.

SPOT THE DIFFERENCE

Jaguars are often confused with leopards, but they live on different continents and are heavier. There is also a difference in their spotty coats. Both jaguars and leopards have a spotty, rosette pattern, but the inside of the rosettes aren't the same. Jaguars have a few smaller spots inside the rosettes, leopards don't.

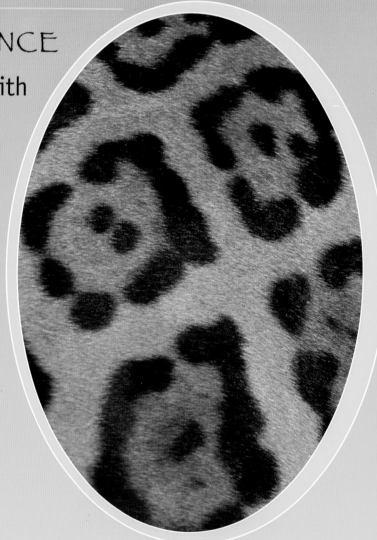

I CAN HEAR YOU

Jaguars are one of the few members of the cat family which can roar. The other big cats which roar are lions, tigers and the jaguars' close relatives, leopards.

Tribespeople often called the jaguar 'the beast which kills its prey with one bound'.

POWERFUL SPIRITS

Some of the ancient *indigenous* peoples of Central and South America worshipped the jaguar as a god. It was seen as a symbol of power, strength and beauty by the *Aztecs*, the *Olmecs* and the *Maya*.

Cheetahs

The cheetah is the great hunter of the cat world and has developed into a lightning-fast machine. But life is still pretty hard for cheetahs.

Once found throughout Africa, the Middle East and in India, the cheetah is now an endangered species.

FAST CAT

Cheetahs are not only the fastest of the big cats, they are the fastest land animal on the planet. These speedy cats can reach around 100 kilometres per hour. Usually a cheetah will give up chasing after about 20 seconds, though sometimes a chase will last as long as a minute.

SPEEDY BUT WEEDY

The cheetah is quite a lightweight cat, which is great for travelling fast, but bad for fighting. Often a cheetah will catch its prey, only to have it stolen by a bigger, meaner predator such as a lion, hyena or even a baboon.

ROYAL CONNECTIONS

Cheetahs are one of the easiest cats to tame and were once the fashionable pets of ancient royalty. It is believed the cheetahs have been kept as pets for over 5,000 years. Cheetahs were used as hunting cats by royalty. They used the cheetahs' speed to catch other animals.

Cougars

The sleek and athletic cougar is the most common of American big cats. Sadly, it is still legal to hunt the cougar in some parts of America.

WHERE ARE THEY FOUND?

Cougars are found from southern Canada right down to Patagonia in South America. However, cougar groups are becoming isolated by new housing developments.

FACE TO FACE

If you ever meet a cougar, the trick is to make yourself look as big as possible and stare the cougar straight in the eye. Don't bend down – that would make you look small and edible!

BURIED TREASURE

The cougar doesn't hide its food in trees like the leopard – instead, it buries it under a pile of leaves and dirt. The cougar returns to it every night until it's all gone.

PAIN IN THE NECK

Cougars will eat almost anything from deer and beaver to insects. Cougars like to sneak up on their prey, and then pounce on it. They then break their prey's neck with a bite from their powerful jaws.

Cougars are also called puma, mountain lion and Florida panther.

21

Glossary

Aztecs (also Olmecs and Maya)
People of ancient civilisations in Central and South America

Camouflage
A pattern designed to make it hard to see something against a background

Carnivore
Creatures that eat meat – that is, other creatures!

Environment
The surroundings of an animal with all the things that affect its life

Extinction
Reduction of numbers to the point that an entire population dies out

Habitat
The place where an animal prefers to live, such as rainforest or plain

Indigenous
Belonging to a place, having been there for a very long time

Poachers
People who hunt animals illegally

Predator
An animal that catches, kills and eats other animals

Prey
Animal killed by another for food

Sabre
A kind of long, curved sword

Species
A group of similar plants or animals

Further Reading

Big Cats
Jonathan Sheikh-Miller and Stephanie Turnbull, Usborne Publishing (Usborne Discovery series), 2008

My Best Book of Big Cats
Christiane Gunzi, Kingfisher Books, 2006

Big Cats
Sarah Walker, Dorling Kindersley (Eye Wonder series), 2005

Big Cats: Hunters of the Night
Elaine Landau, Enslow Publishers Inc. (Animals After Dark series), 2007

Big Cat Diary: Leopard
Jonathan and Angela Scott, Collins, 2006

Wild Cats
Therese Shea, PowerKids Press (Big Bad Biters series), 2006